what about... how we live?

what about... how we live?

Brian Williams

First published in 2004 by Miles Kelly Publishing Ltd
Bardfield Centre, Great Bardfield Essex CM7 4SL

This edition printed in 2008 by Miles Kelly Publishing Ltd

4 6 8 10 9 7 5 3

British Library Cataloguing-in-Publication Data
A catalogue record for this book is available from the British Library

ISBN 978-1-84236-788-9

Printed in Thailand

Editorial Director Belinda Gallagher
Art Director Jo Brewer
Senior Editor Jenni Rainford
Assistant Editors Lucy Dowling, Teri Mort
Copy Editor Rosalind Beckman
Design Concept John Christopher
Volume Designers Jo Brewer, Michelle Cannatella
Picture Researcher Liberty Newton
Indexer Helen Snaith
Production Manager Elizabeth Brunwin
Reprographics Anthony Cambray, Stephan Davis, Liberty Newton, Ian Paulyn

www.mileskelly.net
info@mileskelly.net

www.factsforprojects.com

CONTENTS

CONTENTS

MUSIC

People have played and listened to music ever since Stone Age cave-dwellers banged drums and shook rattles. Throughout the centuries, instruments were refined and developed, and the skills needed to play them were taught to others. Music has been written down only since about 1800 BC. A huge variety of different musical styles has been developed across the world, including classical, opera, folk, reggae, jazz, soul, rock and pop.

What are the four main groups of instruments?

The main groups of instruments are wind, stringed, percussion and brass. Wind and brass instruments are played by blowing down a hollow tube with holes in. Stringed instruments have strings stretched tight across a hollow box; the strings are vibrated with a bow (violin) plucked with the fingers or a plectrum (guitar). Percussion instruments such as drums and cymbals make sounds when struck by hammers, sticks or the hands.

These are examples from three of the musical instrument groups: French horn (brass), violin and guitar (strings) and conga drums (percussion).

Who are the greatest composers?

People may never agree on 'the greatest-ever composer', but many music-lovers place Wolfgang Amadeus Mozart (1756–91), Ludwig van Beethoven (1770–1827) and Johann Sebastian Bach (1685–1750) among their favourites. Notable works by these musical geniuses include Bach's *Brandenburg Concertos*, Beethoven's *Ode to Joy* and *5th Symphony*, and Mozart's *Eine Kleine Nachtmusik*.

All three composers wrote music for small groups of musicians as well as for full orchestras.

Making **music**

Key **dates**

Invented	
c. 4000 BC	Flute, harp, trumpet
3500 BC	Bells
AD 1500	Trombone
c.1545	Violin
1709	Piano
1821	Harmonica
1822	Accordion
1832	Modern flute
1840	Saxophone

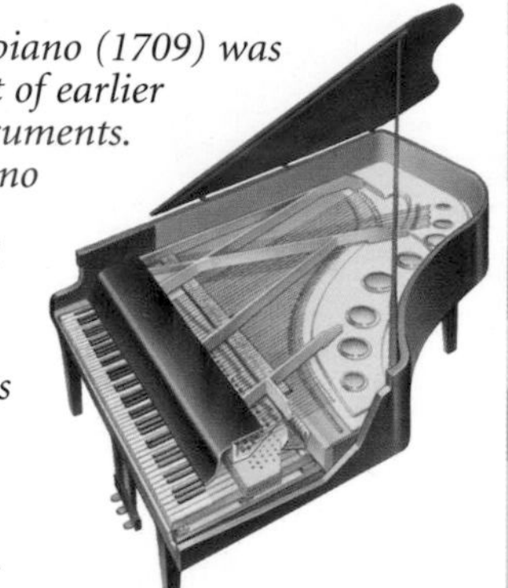

The grand piano (1709) was a development of earlier keyboard instruments. The grand piano (1855) is normally used in orchestral concerts. Upright pianos and electronic keyboards are used for other types of music.

Star **performers**

Name	Nationality	Music
Maria Callas (1923–77)	Greek	soprano singer
Enrico Caruso (1873–1921)	Italian	tenor singer
Ella Fitzgerald (1918–96)	American	jazz singer
Madonna (born 1958)	American	popular singer
Luciano Pavarotti (born 1935)	Italian	tenor singer
Elvis Presley (1935–77)	American	rock'n'roll singer
Frank Sinatra (1915–98)	American	popular singer
Stevie Wonder (born 1950)	American	popular singer

Who were the first successful rock stars?

The first rock superstar was Elvis Presley, who had 94 gold singles and more than 40 gold albums. Then in the 1960s, the Beatles began their career, which made them the biggest-selling group of all time. The first solo singer to sell one million records was the opera singer Enrico Caruso. Until the 20th century, popular songs were only heard when people sang or played them 'live'. Recorded sound, which dates from the 1880s, changed the way people listened to music, and radio and the record industry combined to create the 'pop' industry, which began in the 1940s with the creation of the first popular hit charts.

The Beatles from left to right: Paul McCartney, Ringo Starr, George Harrison and John Lennon.

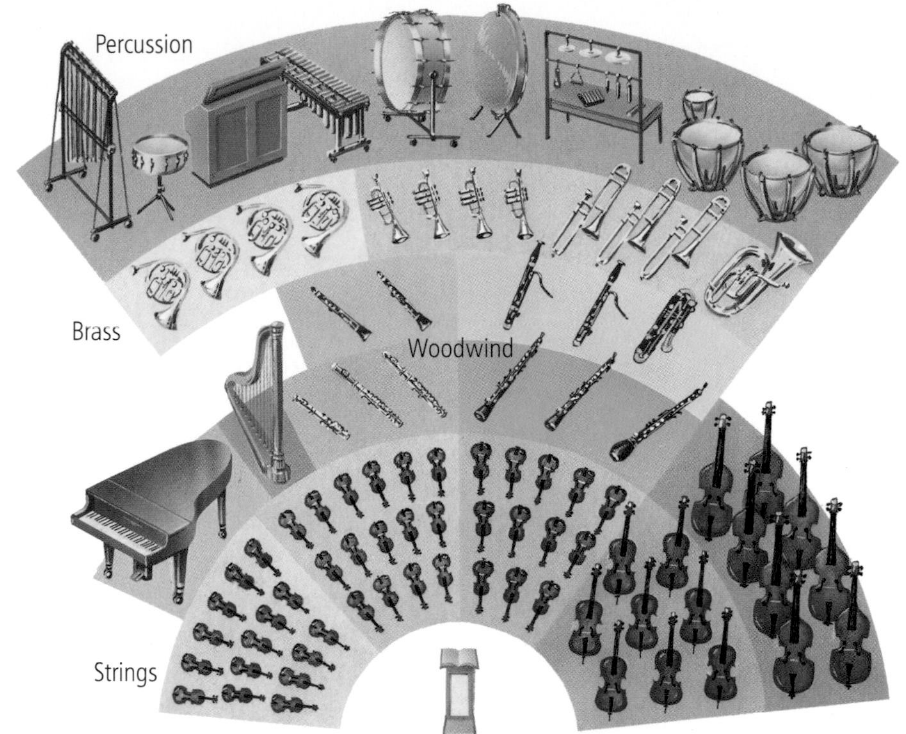

The instruments of the symphony orchestra are arranged in groups in an arc in front of the conductor – strings at the front, then wind, and percussion at the back.

Who wrote the longest opera?

The five longest operas (all lasting more than five hours) were written by the 19th-century German composer Richard Wagner. The longest of Wagner's operas is *The Twilight of the Gods*. An opera is a play in which the actors sing as they act, and in which music plays a much more important part than plot, dialogue or set. Operas were first staged around 1600 in Italy.

How many instruments make up an orchestra?

The modern orchestra has about 100 musicians. Orchestras have four main sections: woodwind (clarinets, flutes, oboes and bassoons), brass (horns and trumpets), percussion (drums, cymbals and bells) and strings (violins, violas, cellos and double basses). The biggest orchestra of all time had 987 instruments and was assembled in 1872 in Boston, USA.

Great **composers**

Johann Sebastian Bach (1685–1750) – German baroque composer.
Ludwig van Beethoven (1770–1827) – German classical composer.
Johannes Brahms (1833–97) – German romantic composer.
Benjamin Britten (1913–76) – British 20th-century composer.
Frederick Chopin (1841–1904) – Polish romantic composer.
Edward Elgar (1857–1934) – British classical composer.
George Gershwin (1898–1937) – American 20th-century composer.
Edvard Grieg (1843–1907) – Norwegian 19th-century composer.
George Frideric Handel (1685–1759) – German/British baroque composer.
Joseph Haydn (1732–1809) – Austrian classical composer.
Wolfgang Amadeus Mozart (1756–91) – Austrian classical composer, who wrote more than 40 symphonies.
Franz Peter Schubert (1797–1828) – Austrian classical and romantic composer.
Igor Stravinsky (1882–1971) – Russian 20th-century modernist composer, most celebrated work, *The Rite of Spring.*
Peter Ilyich Tchaikovsky (1840–93) – Russian romantic composer, famous for symphonies and ballet scores.
Giuseppe Verdi (1813–1901) – Italian 19th century opera composer.
Richard Wagner (1818–83) – German romantic composer.

ART

The earliest art was made by Stone Age people, who painted pictures on walls and made figures from stone and clay. There are many kinds of art – from famous paintings sold for many millions of pounds at auction to clay pots made by children in school. Art can puzzle as well as astound. Some artists have wrapped cliffs in plastic, covered buildings in cloth, displayed a bed with dirty washing, put a dead animal in a case and cut away half a mountain in their efforts to create a unique piece.

What does a sculptor do?

Sculptors are artists who make models, such as figures carved in wood or stone, or cast in metal. The two most common techniques in sculpture are carving and moulding. Modern sculptors also create art from assembling pieces of scrap, plastic or even paper. A figure of the native Indian known as Crazy Horse being cut into the rock of Thunderhead Mountain in South Dakota, USA (still not finished after over 50 years) will be 172 m high when it is completed.

Who was Picasso?

Picasso was one of the most successful painters of the 20th century. His full name was Pablo Ruiz y Picasso; he was born in Spain in 1881 and died in 1973. He began by painting in a traditional, realistic style but then began depicting figures as fragments of geometric shapes – this style became known as Cubism. One of his most famous pictures is called *Guernica* and portrays the suffering of people during the Spanish Civil War in the 1930s.

➔ *Picasso was a prolific artist who worked on canvas in several styles. Unlike many other artists, Picasso also earned a lot of money from his work.*

➔ The Venus de Milo *is one of the most famous sculptures. This Roman copy of the Greek original is in The Louvre museum in Paris.*

What is ceramics?

Ceramics is the art of making fine pottery, using clay. Potters have made everyday items such as beakers and plates for more than 5,000 years. Examples of pottery are earthenware bowls, Greek and Chinese vases, and terracotta heads and figures. Painted and glazed porcelain (the most delicate form of pottery) was first made in China about 1,300 years ago.

➔ *Porcelain vases were made in China during the period known as the Ming dynasty (1368–1644), when the arts flourished.*

World of **art**

Key **dates**

1266–1337 Giotto, Italian, his pictures showed people in a more lifelike way.

1452–1519 Leonardo da Vinci, Italian, painter, sculptor and architect, famous for the *Mona Lisa*.

1475–1564 Michelangelo Buionarotti, Italian, painted Rome's Sistine Chapel ceiling.

1483–1520 Raphael, Italian painter who also worked in Rome.

1541–1614 El Greco, Spanish, painted many religious scenes.

➔ *Self-portrait by Rembrandt.*

1606–69 Rembrandt von Rijn, Dutch, master of portraits.

1775–1851 J. M. W. Turner, English, painted mostly landscapes.

1776–1837 John Constable, English, famous for his landscapes.

1840–1926 Claude Monet, French, Impressionist, famous for paintings of his garden and various landscape scenes.

1853–90 Vincent van Gogh, Dutch, landscapes and portraits.

1881–1973 Pablo Picasso, Spanish, styles included abstract Cubism.

↑ *Wall paintings like this are found in the tombs of Egyptian kings and queens. This picture shows a hunting scene beside the River Nile. Cave paintings depict life at the time of their creation, more than 15,000 years ago.*

What is a fresco?

A fresco is a painting on a wall. In ancient Egypt, teams of master artists worked on large wall paintings. Different minerals were used to make different colours – carbon for black, ochre for red and yellow, and azurite and malachite for green and blue. During the Middle Ages and the Renaissance, frescoes were a favourite form of decoration in Europe. Fresco artists paint on fresh plaster while it is wet, so they have to work fast. They begin by drawing a sketch, from which they trace the outline on the plaster, and then brush in the colours. As the plaster dries and hardens, the colours are bonded to the wall.

What kind of paints did cave painters use?

The paints used by cave painters, more than 12,000 years ago, were made from everyday materials, such as coloured soil, clay, animal fat, soot and charcoal from their fires and the roots of plants. They painted the animals they hunted, such as ibex, wild ox and deer. The artists did not use brushes but painted with their fingers, sometimes leaving an impression of their hands, perhaps as a signature.

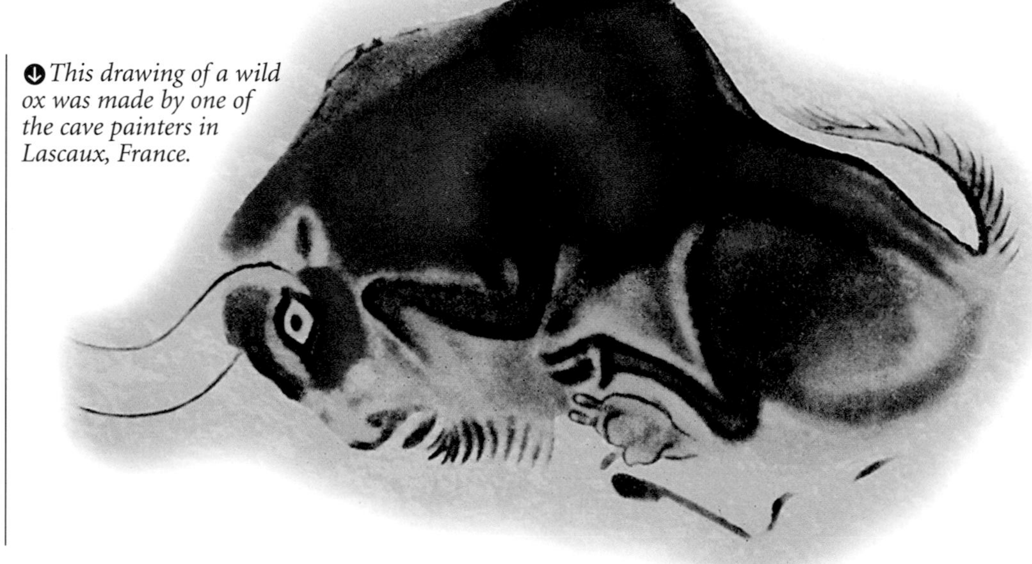

↓ *This drawing of a wild ox was made by one of the cave painters in Lascaux, France.*

Modern **artists**

Alexander Calder (1898–1976) – American sculptor of mobiles.

Christo (born 1935) – Bulgarian-born Belgian, famous for wrapping buildings and sections of coastline in plastic.

Salvador Dali (1904–89) – Spanish Surrealist painter.

Barbara Hepworth (1903–75) – British sculptor.

David Hockney (born 1937) – British painter.

Roy Lichtenstein (1923–97) – American pop artist.

Salvador Dali

Henry Moore (1898–1986) – British sculptor.

Piet Mondrian (1872–1944) – Dutch painter of abstracts.

Gilbert and George (Gilbert Proesch born 1943 and George Passmore born 1942) – British avant-garde artists known for their 'Performance Art'.

Andy Warhol (1928–87) – American painter and graphic artist famous for prints of soup cans and Marilyn Monroe.

Andy Warhol

DESIGN

Design involves planning, and a designer's job is to create something new, either from brand new materials or by reassembling existing ones. Designers often have to be part-artist, part-engineer and part-salesperson. Some of those whose work includes design are architects, engineers, fashion designers, gardeners, graphic artists (who design books and magazines), interior decorators, stage- and movie-set designers and shop-window dressers.

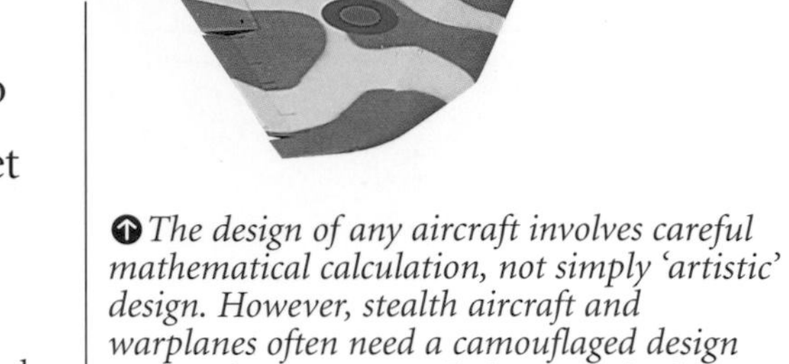

The design of any aircraft involves careful mathematical calculation, not simply 'artistic' design. However, stealth aircraft and warplanes often need a camouflaged design so that they cannot easily be recognized in a dangerous combat situation.

Who designed the pyramids?

The Egyptian architects who built the pyramids were scribes, astronomers and government officials, the most famous of whom was Imhotep. He lived in the 2500s BC and one of his many jobs was court physician to King Djoser. He designed the Step Pyramid at Saggara in Egypt, as a tomb for the king. Architects design buildings by making drawings and doing calculations, but today they also use computers to picture the finished design, to see the inside, and to show how any changes will alter the product.

The only step pyramid ever completed is situated at Saqqara. It was built by King Djoser.

What makes a good design?

There are several principles of design, including balance, repetition, rhythm and unity (overall effect). Design is the basis of every manufacturing process, but however much fun it is to design a complex object, it will not be a success unless it can be manufactured and sold. Design involves arranging materials for a particular or desired effect – either for pleasure or to fulfil a particular function, such as a commission. If a design looks good and works efficiently, people will want to use it. The design of a warplane involves careful mathematical calculation, not simply 'artistic' design. Their strength and safety are just as important as their appearance, which is often camouflaged.

Shaping up **for design**

Craft and design

The term 'designer' dates from the 1600s. Before then, a craftsman who made a chair was both designer and maker. By the 1800s, workers in factories were mass-producing chairs to designs drawn up by specialized designers. The poet and designer William Morris rebelled against factory-produced goods, and started an 'Arts and Crafts' movement in the 1880s, to return to handmade craftsmanship. The first electrical appliances such as vacuum cleaners were unattractive to look at. Today we expect household appliances not only to work well but also to look good in our homes so design is an important feature of manufacturing such products.

The penny-farthing bicycle of the 1870s was an awkward shape, but the bike was actually very fast – even if tricky to get on and off.

Egyptians designed and crafted artefacts with bright symbols and colourful designs.

A Victorian sitting room was designed for people to sit, read, and amuse themselves in.

Who first used furniture?

The first people to use furniture were the ancient Egyptians – we know this because they put chairs, stools and tables in their tombs. Thomas Chippendale wrote the first catalogue about furniture in England in 1754. It had drawings of the pieces he offered for sale, and his designs for chairs, tables and cabinets were widely imitated. A great deal of furniture made in the late 18th century is often described as 'Chippendale', because it describes a style, even though in most cases Chippendale himself was not involved.

Furniture designers copied styles of each other, such as Chippendale, as well as from designers abroad.

What was Victorian style like?

The Victorians were the first people to have factory-made curtains, chairs, carpets and household gadgets and so the style of their homes often looks cluttered to modern eyes. People liked lots of pictures and ornaments, and filled rooms with chairs, tables, lamps, bookcases and shelves. Victorian clothes look thick and heavy to us, and sombre colours were preferred. Queen Victoria's reign lasted from 1837 to 1901, so Victorians lived during a new industrial age.

When did the fashion industry begin?

When factory-made clothes went on sale in the 19th century, poorer people were able to buy cheap copies of fashionable clothes. Previously, wealthy people had always bought elegant clothes and set styles for others to copy. In the 20th century, fashion designers such as Coco Chanel and Christian Dior set up fashion 'houses', designing exclusive designs. In the 1960s–70s, youth fashion became the rage, and today designers and super-models rival pop and movie stars as world-famous celebrities.

In the 19th century, the clothes worn by wealthy women were copied by new fashion houses, who supplied cheap clothes to poorer people.

The Petronas Towers in Kuala Lumpur, Malaysia, were designed to impress people with their grand height. The tower was built 88 storeys high and the designers shaped each of the floors like an eight-pointed star. At the 50th floor is a glass-covered bridge. Though no longer the world's tallest building, the Petronas Towers did hold the record for a number of years.

Indonesian long-houses are designed and built in a traditional style.

Bagless vacuum

James Dyson, who trained as a furniture designer, invented the bagless cleaner. He first had the idea in 1978 and spent five years making and testing more than 5,000 prototypes. Dyson's factory started making bagless cleaners in 1993.

The dyson is designed for use without a reusable bag.

ARCHITECTURE

Architecture is the art and science of designing and constructing buildings. The architect has to consider the look, the technology, the site and the cost of the building. Much of early architecture comprised monumental temples, tombs and palaces. The Greeks introduced 'classical' rules of proportion and, ever since, architectural style has reflected the tastes of the age in which it is used.

When did the Greeks build temples?

Greek architecture began to take shape about 600 BC. The beauty of the Parthenon temple on the Acropolis hill in Athens typifies Greek architecture. The Greeks loved harmonious proportions. The roofs of their graceful buildings were supported by columns built in three main styles, known as Doric, Ionic and Corinthian, which became more decorative as time passed.

Where were the first skyscrapers built?

The first skyscrapers were built in the American city of Chicago after a fire in 1871 destroyed many of its buildings. The first skyscraper was the 10-storey Home Insurance Building. Developments that made skyscrapers possible included the use of steel girders to support tall buildings internally, and the invention of the electric lift, which meant that people did not have to use stairs to reach the upper floors.

The Parthenon was built between 447 and 432 BC, using classic principles of geometry.

Many skyscrapers, like these in Hong Kong, China, have more than 200 storeys. Plans are continually made to build higher and higher.

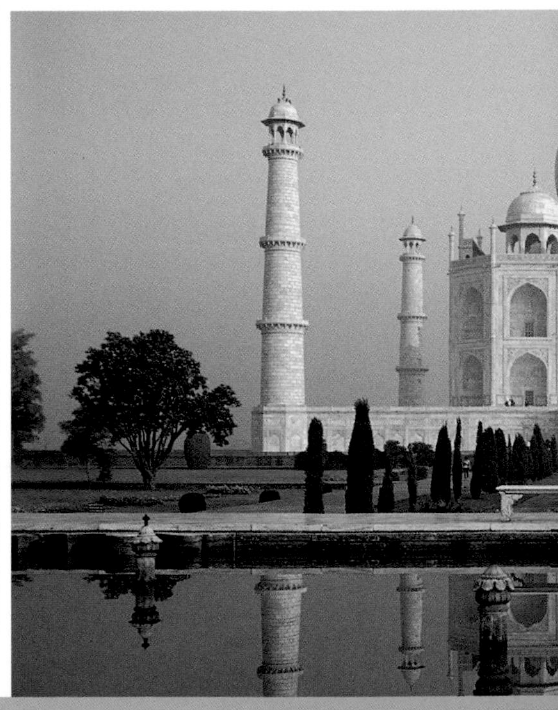

Skyline shapers

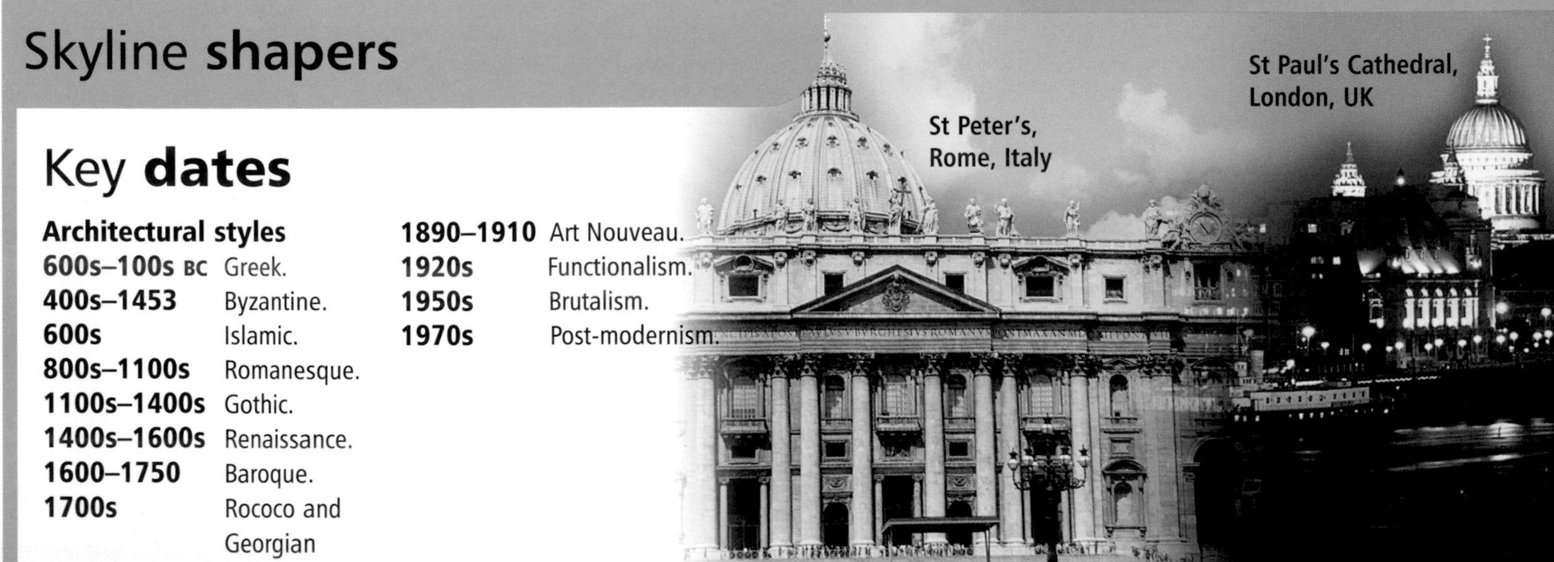

Key dates

Architectural styles

600s–100s BC	Greek.
400s–1453	Byzantine.
600s	Islamic.
800s–1100s	Romanesque.
1100s–1400s	Gothic.
1400s–1600s	Renaissance.
1600–1750	Baroque.
1700s	Rococo and Georgian
1890–1910	Art Nouveau.
1920s	Functionalism.
1950s	Brutalism.
1970s	Post-modernism.

What is the world's most impressive building?

Many would suggest the Taj Mahal in India. The Mogul ruler of India, Shah Jahan, built the Taj Mahal for his favourite wife, Mumtaz Mahal, when she died in childbirth in 1629. He wanted her to have the most beautiful tomb in the world. More than 20,000 labourers and artists worked on the Taj Mahal, which took 20 years to complete. The domed building is made of white marble and rests on a sandstone platform.

Each of the Taj Mahal's four minarets is 40 m high. The top of the dome is nearly 61 m above the floor, under which is the vault where Shah Jahan is buried with his wife.

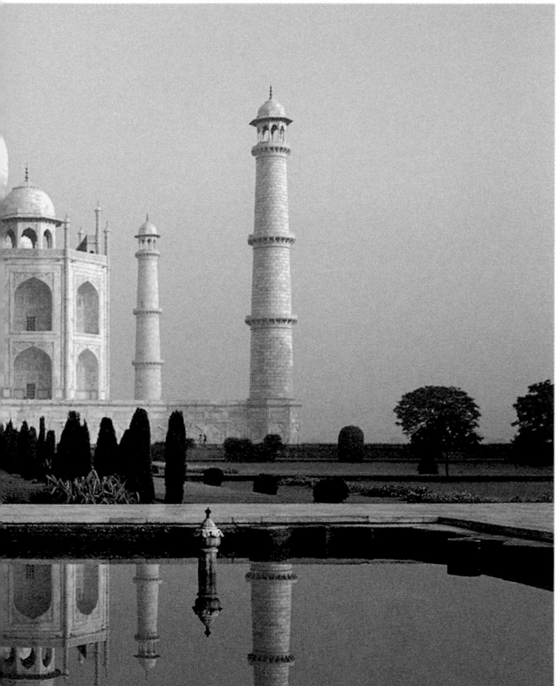

Where is the world's most famous opera house?

Sydney Opera House in Australia has been a world-famous landmark in Sydney Harbour since it was first opened in 1973. An opera house is a theatre, usually devoted to operatic production. Sydney Opera House is used for other events, such as performance art, and has a distinctive design, with a shaped roof that makes it look as if the building is about to set sail across the water. The building was designed by Danish architect, Jorn Lutzon.

When was Stonehenge built?

Stonehenge is a group of huge stones, set in a circle on Salisbury Plain in England, built in stages between 2800 and 1500 BC. The heavy stones were dragged and positioned in alignment with the rising and setting Sun at midsummer. Stonehenge was probably a gathering point and religious centre for local tribal groups.

What is the Louvre?

The Louvre is the national museum of France. It is located in the centre of Paris, and was originally a palace, used since the 1500s by the kings of France to house their art collections. It was first opened to the public in 1793 after the French Revolution. One of the modern features of the Louvre is the steel-and-glass pyramid entrance in the central courtyard, designed by American architect I.M. Pei. It now houses some of the world's finest paintings and works.

The glass pyramid in the courtyard of the Louvre adds a new dimension to an old building.

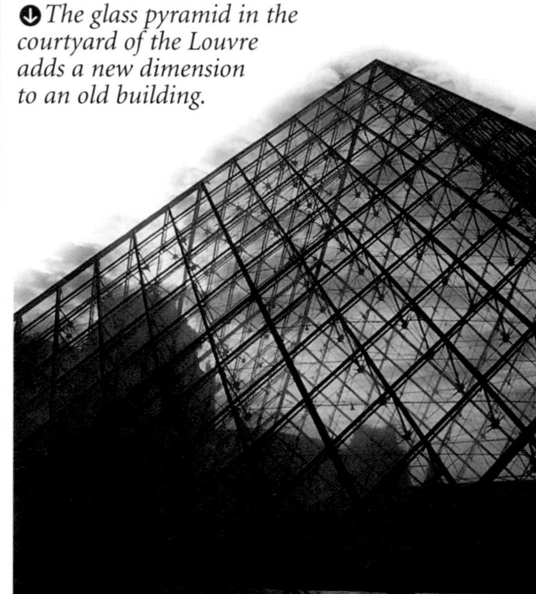

The ancient stones of Stonehenge: some stones have fallen or been removed since the circle was first erected.

The Duomo, Florence, Italy

Famous **architects**

Gianlorenzo Bernini (1598–1680) – Italian, rebuilt St Peter's, Rome.
Filippo Brunelleschi (1377–1446) – Italian, designed the dome of the Duomo in Florence.
Norman Foster (born 1935) – English, designed the Millennium Bridge in London.
Antoni Gaudi (1852–1926) – Spanish, Barcelona structures.
Walter Gropius (1883–1969) – German, refounded the Bauhaus (School of Building).
William le Baron Jenney (1832–1907) – American, designed the first iron-framed skyscraper in Chicago.
Sir Christopher Wren (1632–1723) – English, designed St Paul's Cathedral and Greenwich Hospital.
Frank Lloyd Wright (1869–1959) – American, known for office buildings and his 'prairie houses'.

The performing arts include performances by dancers, musicians, singers, actors and even puppets. Through these varied art forms, storytellers have long thrilled audiences, who have enjoyed the emotional experience of a 'show', whether it be comedy (humour) or tragedy (serious) or a mixture of the two.

The modern circus clown developed from 'buffoons' who performed in Greek and Roman plays, sometimes throwing items such as nuts at the audience!

Which country is most famous for its ballet?

Russia, as it has produced many fine dancers, including Vaslav Nijinsky, Rudolf Nureyev and Anna Pavlova, as well as famous ballet companies, who perform all over the world. However, ballet did not begin in Russia. It was first recognized as an art-form in the 1600s in France, and it was then that the five basic ballet positions were devised. Famous ballets include *Giselle*, *Swan Lake* and *Sleeping Beauty*.

Steps in classical ballet use turn-out (feet pointing sideways) and pointe-work (dancing on tip-toes). Ballet dancers' must be very fit and their muscles extemely strong.

How old are puppet performances?

Puppets are one of the earliest forms of performing entertainment. String puppets, also known as marionettes, have been popular for centuries. One of the traditions of the English seaside resort is the Punch and Judy show, performed by an entertainer who is concealed inside a cubicle using just his hands (inside glove puppets) and his voice. Other puppets have become famous as television celebrities in their own right, and some of the computer-generated figures have become almost life-like. In Indonesia people watch plays performed by 'shadow-puppets'.

When did the first circus appear?

In ancient Rome a circus was called a stadium. In the 1700s, showmen used the name 'circus' for horse shows in Europe. Philip Astley put on shows of trick-riding in the 1770s in London. Travelling circuses, which often included horses, wild animals, acrobats and clowns, became popular in the 1800s. The most famous circus is Ringling Brothers and Barnum and Bailey's (the two shows combined in 1919), which had the biggest ever Big Top (tent).

Writer and **players**

Backstage at the theatre

To perform a play in a theatre, it takes more people than the actors. Behind the scenes a team of backstage technicians work hard to ensure that every theatre performance is well-organized and seamless. Set-designers, costume organizers, lighting technicians, sound monitors, curtain technicians – even ticket sales staff are all crucial to the success of a performance.

William Shakespeare's plays were first performed in the original open-air Globe Theatre, which has been recreated beside the River Thames in London.

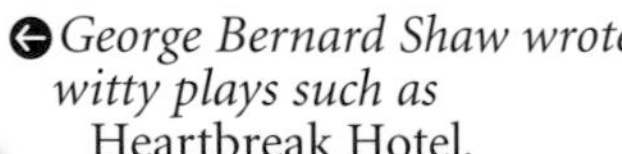

George Bernard Shaw wrote witty plays such as Heartbreak Hotel.

Anton Chekhov is Russia's most celebrated dramatist. He is best known for his tragedies.

Who was the most famous silent comedian?

One of the most famous cinema stars was Charlie Chaplin (1889–1977). He was was also one of the first movie-stars. Chaplin learnt his craft as a comedian on the music-hall stage in London but then went to America where he made his name as a comic actor in silent movies. His success as a comedian has made him synonomous with silent movies.

Charlie Chaplin's character 'little man' in baggy trousers, with a bowler hat and cane, became known all over the world.

Greeks sat in open-air theatres to watch one of two types of play: tragedies or comedies. Tragedies were serious plays and included a sad end, an unhappy love affair, a crime or a disaster. Comedies were humorous plays. Traditionally, tragedy and comedy were never mixed.

Fancy dress and masks are a feature of the carnival in Venice.

What is a carnival?

The original carnival was a religious holiday and feast, celebrated before the beginning of the Christian fasting period of Lent. The modern carnival is a huge outdoor theatre and parade, with dancers, decorated floats, entertainers and marching bands. Famous carnivals are held in Brazil, the USA and the UK.

Who went to the first theatres?

The first theatre-goers were the ancient Greeks, who gathered in hundreds and sat on hillsides to watch tragedies and comedies. Greek theatres were bowl-shaped arenas, surrounding a circular stage, called an orchestra. The Romans built stone theatres that could seat 40,000 to watch raucous comedies. The most successful playwright in the world is the English bard William Shakespeare (1564–1616), whose plays are staged all over the world and whose Globe Theatre has been recreated in London.

Famous **playwrights**

Aristophanes (c. 445–385 BC) – Greek, wrote comedies such as *The Frogs.*

Alan Ayckbourne (born 1939) – British, prolific author of successful comedies of modern life, including *The Norman Conquests.*

Samuel Becket (1906–89) – Irish, wrote *Waiting for Godot.*

Anton Chekhov (1860–1904) – Russian, wrote *The Cherry Orchard.*

William Congreve (1670–1729) – English, author of *The Way of the World*, a comedy.

Johann Wolfgang von Goethe (1749–1832) – German, playwright and scientist, his most famous work is *Faust,* in which a scholar sells his soul to the devil.

Henrik Ibsen (1828–1906) – Norwegian, wrote *A Dolls House* and *Hedda Gabbler.*

Molière (Jean-Baptiste Poquelin) (1622–73) – French, wrote comedies including *The Misanthropist* and *The Miser.*

Eugene O'Neill (1888–1953) – American, wrote *The Iceman Cometh* and other plays.

William Shakespeare (1564–1616) – English, greatest dramatist whose plays include tragedies (*King Lear*), comedies (*Much Ado About Nothing*) and histories (*Julius Caesar*)

George Bernard Shaw (1856–1950) – Irish, wrote *St Joan*, *Major Barbara* and other plays, usually from a satirical viewpoint.

Richard Brinsley Sheridan (1751–1816) – Irish, wrote *The Rivals*, one of the most enduring comedies.

Sophocles (about 496–406 BC) – Greek, wrote tragedies, including *Oedipus the King.*

Tom Stoppard (Thomas Straussler, born 1937) – Czech-born British writer, whose plays include *Travesties* and *Jumpers.*

Cinema was made possible by the invention of the camera obscura and lantern slide, which projected pictures onto a screen. By the 1930s, millions of people visited the cinema every week. The advent of television in the 1950s, however, enabled more people to stay at home to watch TV and video movies on 'the box'. Now DVD (digital versatile disc) provides us with home entertainment unimagined by early pioneers of screen entertainment.

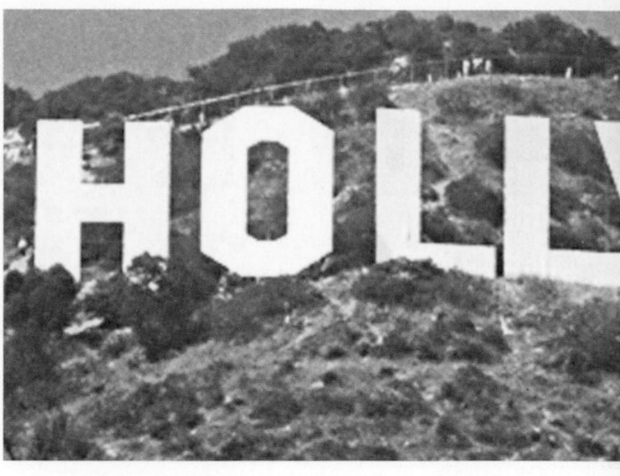

How did 'movies' develop?

Moving images, known as 'movies' developed in the early 1900s, after experiments with 'kinetoscope' peepshows. The first big movie was D. W. Griffith's epic *Birth of a Nation* in 1915. Early movies were silent and dialogue appeared as words printed on the screen. Often a pianist played appropriate music in the cinema. 'Talkies' appeared in the late 1920s.

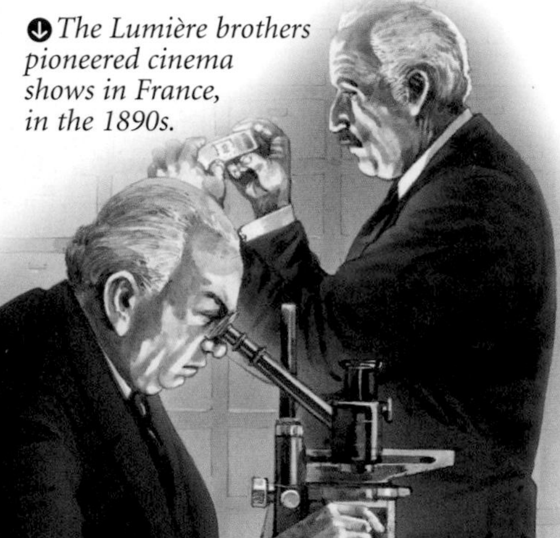

The Lumière brothers pioneered cinema shows in France, in the 1890s.

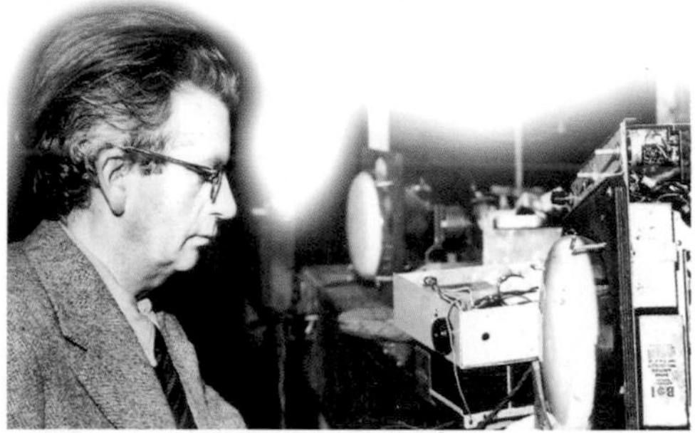

John Logie Baird was a pioneer of television.

When did people first watch TV?

The first TV pictures were produced in 1924 by John Logie Baird, but a more effective electronic system was used for the first BBC TV service in 1936. When the television age began, very few people owned sets, and pictures were in flickering black-and-white. Today, satellite and cable networks provide hundreds of channels around the world, with thousands of hours of viewing.

Where is the centre of the movie industry?

Although the cinema was a French invention, thanks largely to the Lumière brothers, it was America that gave birth to the international movie industry. Movie-makers found that sunny California was an ideal place to shoot movies, and by the 1920s Hollywood had become 'the capital of the motion picture world', with large studios full of technicians, writers, make-up artists, costume designers, set-builders, producers and directors.

Modern TV cameras work in any conditions. Today, TV is the world's biggest medium for information and in-home entertainment.

Movie **magic**

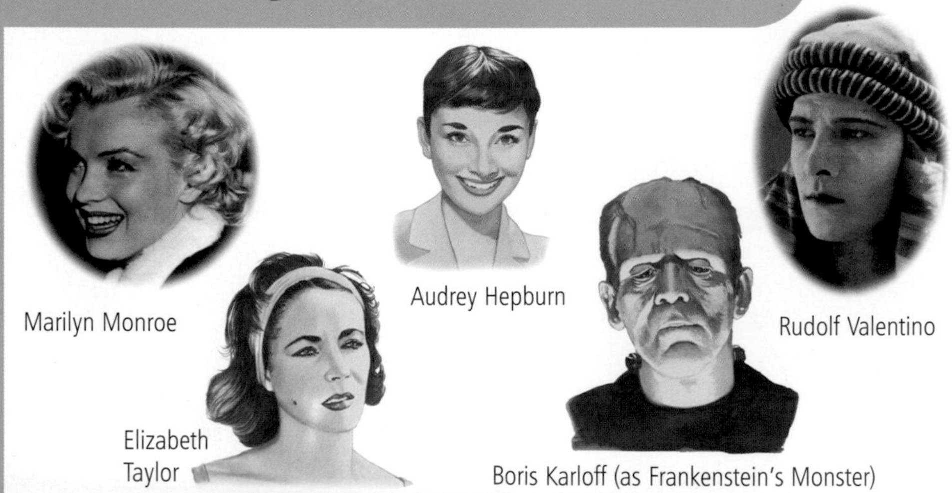

Movie **terms**

Dubbing – Adding words to pictures.
Flash-back – Interruption in the story to recall a past event.
Long shot – A picture taken from a distance.
Prop – Short for 'property', an object used by an actor, such as a weapon or a mobile phone.
Rushes – Shots taken during a day's filming, before editing.
Shooting – Filming a scene.
Take – Part of a scene, with words and action, shot without interruption.

The Hollywood sign on the hill tells visitors they have reached the heart of 'movieland'.

What is the difference between a producer and a director?

In the movie industry, a producer raises money to make a new movie and organizes the financial side, while the director is in charge of filming. The director tells the camera crews how to set up their cameras, and directs the actors to act the way the script is written. In TV, however, the producer may also act as the director: the money comes from the TV company who is making the series or programme.

Alfred Hitchcock, director and master of suspense, made a cameo appearance in most of his movies.

Where would you find someone using a clapperboard?

A clapperboard is used in a movie or TV studio to mark the beginning or end of a 'take' (a short section of movie). Movies are not usually made in the order of a story. Director, scriptwriters, camera crew and actors work on the scenes in whatever order is convenient. This might be when the star is available or when the weather is right. Several takes may be needed before a scene is filmed properly. The final takes are put together in order by an editor and, if necessary, cut to create the finished movie.

Details of each take are filled in on the clapperboard, which is held up in front of the camera before filming begins.

Special effects, such as those used in the Matrix (US 2000), create excitement in a movie and allow scenes to be created that would otherwise be difficult, dangerous or impossible.

The Oscars

Oscars are the gold-plated awards presented each year by the US Academy of Motion Picture Arts and Sciences. Katharine Hepburn (1907–2003) is the only actor to have won four Oscars.

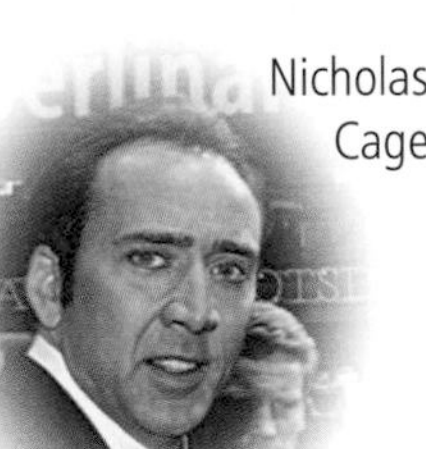

Nicholas Cage

Samuel Jackson

Nicole Kidman

Tom Cruise

George Clooney

Oscar-winning **movies**

Date	Movie
1994	*Forrest Gump*
1995	*Braveheart*
1996	*The English Patient*
1997	*Titanic*
1998	*Shakespeare in Love*
1999	*American Beauty*
2000	*Gladiator*
2001	*Crouching Tiger, Hidden Dragon*
2002	*The Lord of the Rings: the Two Towers*
2003	*Chicago*
2004	*The Lord of the Rings: the Return of the King*

The earliest literature was oral (spoken word or song) not written. The oldest hand-printed book dates from the AD 800s, but books were not available cheaply until the invention of steam-powered printing machines in the 1800s. Paperbacks were produced from the 1930s. The most quoted writer is William Shakespeare, and the most widely read children's books of today are the adventures of Harry Potter, by British author, J. K. Rowling.

What is an illuminated manuscript?

A manuscript, or hand-written book, was either hand-printed (using a wood block) or copied by hand by monks, who decorated the pages with beautifully coloured illuminations. Often the monks began a page with a decorated letter. Before the printing press with movable type was invented in the 1440s, monks did most of the book copying in Europe. Today, ancient illuminated manuscripts, such as the *Book of Kells* and the *Lindisfarne Gospels*, are priceless treasures.

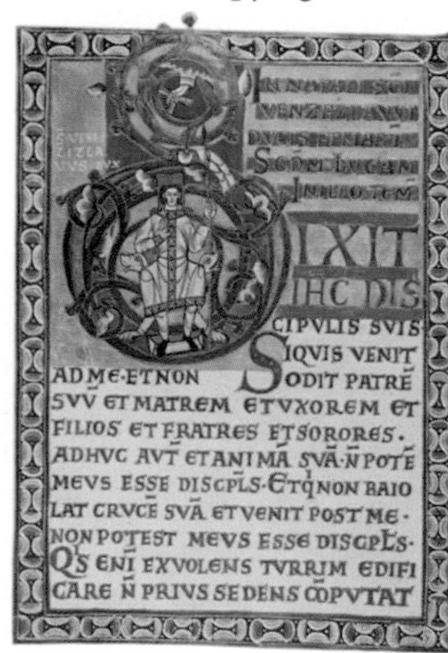
DIXIT
IHC DIS
CIPVLIS SVIS
SIQVIS VENIT
AD ME ET NON ODIT PATRE
SVV ET MATREM ET VXOREM ET
FILIOS ET FRATRES ET SORORES.
ADHVC AVT ET ANIMA SVA N POTE
MEVS ESSE DISCPLS ET Q NON BAIO
LAT CRVCE SVA ET VENIT POST ME
NON POTEST MEVS ESSE DISCPLS.
QS ENI EX VOLENS TVRRIM EDIFI
CARE N PRIVS SEDENS COPVTAT

Medieval illuminated manuscripts took such a long time to make, because they were hand-written, that they had to be treated with great care.

Who was the most famous fictional detective?

Sherlock Holmes, the pipe-smoking master-sleuth, created by British writer Sir Arthur Conan Doyle (1859–1930). Holmes and his friend Dr Watson solved mysteries involving mysterious dogs (*The Hound of the Baskervilles*), venomous snakes (*The Speckled Band*) and numerous robberies and murders. He was eventually 'killed off' in a final contest with his arch-enemy, the criminal genius Professor Moriarty, but was then 'reborn' by popular demand.

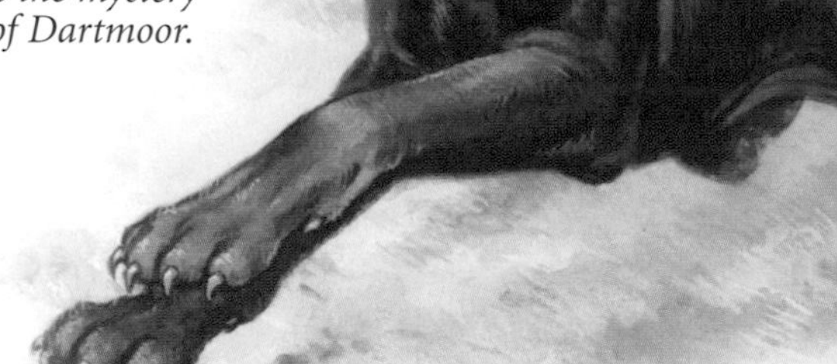

In The Hound of the Baskervilles, *Sherlock Holmes investigates the mystery of the legendary hellhound of Dartmoor.*

Which famous novelist gave public readings of his work?

Charles Dickens (1812–70), a talented amateur actor, gave public performances of scenes from his best-selling novels. Dickens is considered one of the greatest British novelists, writing a succession of masterpieces including *Oliver Twist* (1838), *Nicholas Nickleby* (1839), *David Copperfield* (1850) and *Great Expectations* (1861).

Dickens endured hard times as a child, which he never forgot, even when he became a successful author.

Books, authors and **characters**

Key **dates**

1340–1400 Geoffrey Chaucer, English poet, wrote *The Canterbury Tales.*

1547–1616 Miguel de Cervantes, Spanish novelist, wrote *Don Quixote.*

1608–74 John Milton, English poet, wrote *Paradise Lost.*

1667–1705 Jonathan Swift, Irish author, wrote *Gulliver's Travels.*

1770–1850 William Wordsworth, English poet, lead Romantic Movement.

1775–1817 Jane Austen, English novelist, wrote *Pride and Prejudice.*

1788–1824 Lord George Byron, English poet, wrote *Don Juan.*

1795–1821 John Keats, English poet, wrote *Ode to Autumn.*

1805–75 Hans Christian Andersen, Danish, wrote many fairy tales.

1821–81 Fyodor Dostoyevsky, Russian novelist, wrote *Crime and Punishment.*

1835–1910 Mark Twain, American author, wrote *Tom Sawyer* and *Huckleberry Finn.*

1840–1928 Thomas Hardy, English novelist, wrote *Tess of the D'Urbervilles.*

1850–94 Robert Louis Stevenson, Scottish author, wrote *Treasure Island.*

1882–1941 James Joyce, Irish author, wrote *Ulysses.*

In Lewis' imaginative story-telling, Alice meets the Mad Hatter, the March Hare and the Dormouse at a very strange tea party.

What was Lewis Carroll's most famous work?

Alice in Wonderland. Lewis Carroll (Charles Lutwidge Dodgson 1832–98) had a shy exterior, but this English mathematician at Oxford University had a wild imagination and delighted in word play. He enjoyed telling stories to friends' children, and wrote two classic children's books: *Alice in Wonderland* (1865) and *Alice Through the Looking Glass* (1872).

Anne Frank died in a concentration camp in 1945. Her father, who survived the death camps, published her diary after the war.

Which teenage girl kept a wartime diary?

Anne Frank, a German teenager living in hiding and in fear of her life, wrote a diary that is regarded as a moving testament to those who died in the Holocaust during World War II (1939–45). Anne's family were Jews who fled Germany to escape persecution by the Nazis. They moved to the Netherlands, but after the Germans invaded in 1940 found themselves in peril once more. Anne, her sister, parents and four friends hid in a secret annexe at the back of an office building. She kept a diary, recording her thoughts until 1944, when the Franks and their friends were discovered and arrested.

Who were Britain's most famous literary sisters?

The Brontës were three sisters who grew up in the village of Haworth, in Yorkshire, with their brother and father, a clergyman. All three became novelists, at first sending in their work under men's names. Charlotte Brontë (1816–55) wrote *Jane Eyre*, about a governess; Emily Brontë (1818–48) wrote a passionate romance, *Wuthering Heights*, while the youngest sister Anne (1820–49) was the author of *The Tenant of Wildfell Hall*.

The Brontë sisters (left to right): Anne, Emily and Charlotte.

Famous **authors and characters**

Author	Character	Author	Character
James Barrie	Peter Pan	Hergé	Tintin
L. Frank Baum	The Wizard of Oz	Rudyard Kipling	Mowgli
Enid Blyton	Noddy	C. S. Lewis	Aslan
Raymond Briggs	The Snowman	A. A. Milne	Winnie the Pooh
John Le Carré	George Smiley	Beatrix Potter	Peter Rabbit
Agatha Christie	Miss Marple, Hercule Poirot	J. K. Rowling	Harry Potter
Roald Dahl	The BFG	R. L. Stevenson	Long John Silver
Ian Fleming	James Bond, 007	J. R. R. Tolkien	Frodo the Hobbit
Kenneth Graham	Toad, Rat, Mole and Badger	Jules Verne	Captain Nemo

MYTHS AND LEGENDS

Myths are stories about gods, supernatural beings and the origins of the world. Legends are stories about heroes, strange animals and adventures, which, while not perhaps true in every detail, may be based on real events. Such stories, some very old, are told all over the world.

Who hid inside a wooden horse?

Greek warriors. The story of the wooden horse is found in *The Iliad*, a long poem by Greek poet, Homer. It tells how the Greeks and the Trojans went to war following the abduction of Helen, the wife of a Greek king, by Paris, Prince of Troy. Troy was besieged for ten years, until the Greeks brought about its downfall by a trick. They built a gigantic wooden horse, inside which warriors were concealed. They left the horse outside Troy, and the unknowing Trojans dragged it into their city. At night, the Greek warriors climbed out, opened the city gates and led the invasion on Troy.

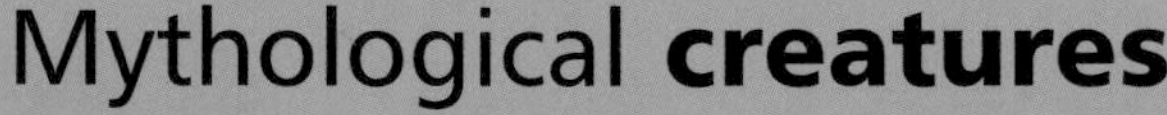

Greek soldiers hid inside a wooden horse as a deception to overthrow the Trojans.

According to legend, Romulus and Remus were cared for and fed by a female wolf.

Who were Romulus and Remus?

Roman legend tells of twins named Romulus and Remus, who founded Rome in 753 BC. As babies, they were thrown into the River Tiber by a wicked uncle, but they were rescued by a she-wolf. Later, a shepherd brought them up. Remus was killed but Romulus became the first king of Rome. The Romans liked legendary explanations; the historical truth is that Rome grew from several village settlements on the seven hills upon which the city stands.

Which people told stories about Ragnarok?

The Vikings and other Norse peoples of Europe. Ragnarok, according to Norse mythology, was a battle between gods, giants and monsters who brought the end of the world. The leader of the gods, one-eyed Odin, led his warriors against his evil enemies from his great hall of Valhalla. In the slaughter, everyone died and the gods' realm of Asgard was destroyed by fire. Yet from this 'twilight of the gods' a new world was born. Two humans who hid in the branches of the World Tree, Yggdrasil, crept out to begin the life-cycle again.

The enemies of the gods rode in a ship with the terrible serpent to the last battle that ended the world.

Mythological creatures

Greek poet Homer wrote The Odyssey, *about the eventful journey of a man called Odysseus, returning home from* The Trojan Wars.

The Amazon warriors also performed rain dances.

Mythological terms

Amazons – A race of women warriors, according to Greek legend.
Aphrodite – Goddess of Love, said to have risen from the sea near Cyprus.
Dragon – Fabulous winged, fire-breathing animal, usually fearsome in Western mythology, but wise and good in Chinese.
Gorgon – Snake-haired monster of Greek myth, whose glance turned people to stone.
Heracles (Hercules) – Famous for his strength, he had to perform 12 'impossible' tasks or labours.

Who led the Argonauts?

The Argonauts, a band of 50 sailors and heroes from Greece, were led by Jason, son of King Aeson. Jason set sail on his ship, the *Argo*, to find the fabulous Golden Fleece – a golden ram's skin hung from a tree and guarded by a fearsome dragon. The Argonauts had many adventures before the arrival of Jason, with the aid of the witch Medea – they defeated the dragon and returned home with the Golden Fleece. The adventures of the Argonauts may have been based on tales told by Greek sailors, exploring the Mediterranean and Black Sea.

One hazard encountered by Jason and the Argonauts on their voyage was the Symplegades – these were rocks that clashed together, crushing everything that passed between them.

Who is Rama?

Rama is one of the gods in Hinduism, the predominent religion of India. He is the hero of an epic poem called the *Ramayana*, written about 2,300 years ago, in Sanskrit (an ancient Indian language often used to write scriptures). It tells how prince Rama wins Sita as his wife, but then has to rescue her from the demon-king, Ravanna, who has kidnapped her and taken her to Lanka (now Sri Lanka). Rama is helped by his brother Laksmana and an army of monkeys.

Why is Anansi the spider so popular?

Anansi is the cunning hero of West African folk tales. He is a 'trickster', living on his quick wits and duping his enemies. Slaves taken from Africa to the United States took Anansi with them, and the stories of the crafty spider probably inspired Brer Rabbit, the hero of the Uncle Remus stories.

Hindus believe that the hero Rama was one of the ten human forms (avatars) of the god Vishnu.

Hiawatha – Mohawk Native American hero, said to have united the tribes and learned the secret of the wilderness.
Lancelot of the Lake – Bravest of the knights of King Arthur.
Mermaid – Sea creatures that looked like beautiful women with tails of fish.
Phoenix – Fabulous bird that was born again from the ashes of its funeral pyre.
Robin Hood – Hero of medieval stories. An English outlaw famous for his skill as an archer.

Legend says that the phoenix was reborn in fire, rising from the flames.

In mythology, the unicorn could only be caught by a maiden.

Unicorn – Mythical animal with a horse's body, a lion's tail and a single horn protruding from its forehead.
Valkyries – Winged maidens in Norse mythology who decided which heroes should die in battle.

HISTORY OF CULTURE

Culture is the way of life of a group of people who share certain customs, beliefs, technology and ideas. People who speak the same language may share the same culture (the Japanese, for example), but not necessarily – English is spoken by people from different cultural backgrounds. Every society has its own culture, and throughout history cultures have borrowed from one another and ideas have been communicated, shared and developed.

When was writing invented?

The earliest form of writing was created some 5,000 years ago in the ruins of Uruk, a city in Sumeria (modern Iraq). It was made by pressing a pointed tool into soft clay. The Sumerians wrote in pictograms (stylized drawings of objects). The ancient Chinese also developed a form of symbol writing using characters to stand for words. By the 1700s, there were over 40,000 Chinese characters! Compared to the 26 letters of the western alphabet, Chinese and its variants are extremely complex.

Which African people were sculptors?

The Nok people of Nigeria, in West Africa, created incredibly detailed and intricate terracotta figures more than 2,500 years ago. The Nok people and the sculptors of Benin (also in West Africa) used a method known as 'lost-wax' to cast bronze. During this process, a wax model is first made, then it is encased in soft clay or wet plaster, which hardens around it to form a mould. The mould is then heated, and the melted wax runs out of a hole, leaving a hollow inside that can be filled with molten bronze. When the bronze has set, the mould is taken apart to reveal the bronze sculpture.

A carved head from West Africa, where craftworkers still make traditional items for the tourist trade.

Which saint became Father Christmas?

St Nicholas, a 5th-century bishop, of whom very little is known except that he probably lived in the area of Asia Minor (modern Turkey). Legends about St Nicholas and tales of his miracles spread and he became a popular saint and Russia's patron saint. In Dutch, Nicholas was known as 'Sinter Claes', and Dutch migrants to America turned him into 'Santa Claus'. In Germany, he became 'Father January' or 'Father Christmas'.

One of the most common legends tells of Father Christmas (Santa Claus) arriving by a sleigh that is drawn by reindeer.

Cultural **history**

Key **dates**

c. 20,000 BC	Cave art and first sculptures.
c. 10,000 BC	First towns, encouraging a settled way of life.
c. 5000–3000 BC	Art and writing developed in Egypt, Mespotamia and China.
2000 BC	Greek and Mycenean art at its height.
400s BC	Golden age of Greek art.
500 BC	Nok culture in Africa.
AD 105	Chinese invent paper.
700	Beginnings of Islamic art. Monastic art in Christian Europe.
1300s–1500s	Renaissance or 'rebirth' of art, learning and new science in Europe.
c. 1440	Invention of printing with movable type.
1600s	First newspapers published in Europe.
1826	Joseph Niepce takes the first photograph, in France.
1876	Alexander Graham Bell demonstrates the telephone.
1885	Benz drives the first car.
1906	Reginald Fessenden demonstrates radio broadcasting.
1927	First 'talkies': cinema films with recorded sound.
1936	BBC starts world's first public television service.
1946	First electronic computer, made in the USA.
1956	Videotape recording introduced.
1960	First communications satellite.

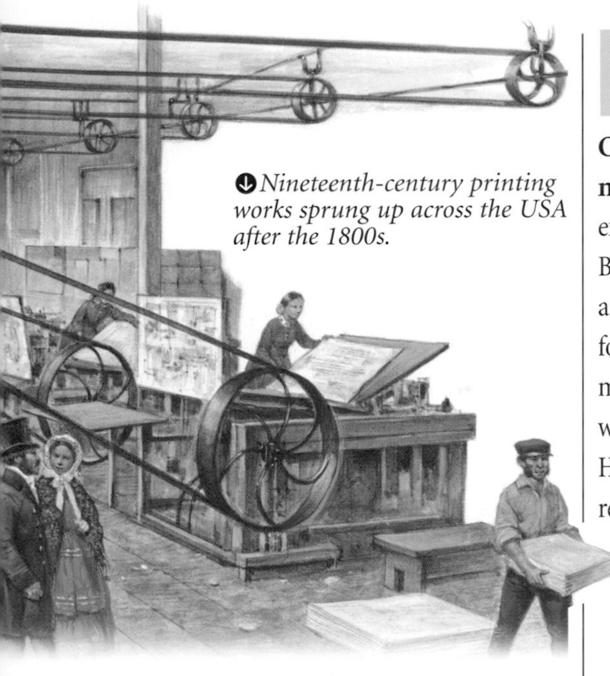

Nineteenth-century printing works sprung up across the USA after the 1800s.

What is oral culture?

Oral culture is passed on by speech, not by being written. In this way, for example, the Celtic people of pre-Roman Britain passed on their history, folk stories and religious beliefs. There was no written form of their language. Oral cultures exist in many parts of the world, and many of the world's epic tales were told in this way. Homer's *Iliad* and *Odyssey* were told and retold by generations of Greeks before they were written down.

Bards or Celtic poets sang to their lord, passing on history, and creating tales about the deeds of current heroes.

It took 700,000 workers 40 years to build the Chinese emperor's tomb and its army of clay soldiers.

How did printing revolutionize culture?

In the 1440s, Johannes Gutenburg invented a screw-press that could print on paper sheets using movable pieces of type, arranged to make words. Printing made books cheaper, but it also brought in standard spellings and punctuation. Books were printed in vernacular (everyday) languages such as English, French and German, and not just in Latin. Novels, magazines and newspapers, even mail-order catalogues were all printed on machines. Knowledge was thus made more widely available to everyone.

Which emperor had clay soldiers in his tomb?

The first emperor of China, Shih Huang-di, who died in 210 BC, was buried with an army of terracotta soldiers and horses. The pharaohs of Egypt were also buried with treasures as well as everyday items. The more important the person, the more splendid the tomb. In many ancient cultures it was the custom to bury 'grave goods' with a dead person for use in the afterlife.

1980s CDs begin to replace magnetized tape for information storage.
1990s Spread of home computers, laptops and World Wide Web via the Internet.
2000s Rapid growth of multi-channel, digital TV and radio and mobile phone networks.

Early alphabets

The use of an alphabet was a key stage in the development of written language. This document in the form of a scroll (an early form of book that rolled up) shows some alphabets. The term alphabet comes from the first two letters of the Greek alphabet, *alpha* and *beta*.

In many countries culture is preserved in folk dance, music and songs.

Snow sports originated in lands where winter snow was prevalent – skiing in Scandinavia, ice-skating on frozen canals in the Netherlands and tobogganing in the Alps. Although ancient Greeks, Romans and Polynesians swam and sailed for pleasure, organized water sports, including swimming and yacht-racing did not develop until the 19th century. Today, winter sports and water sports are included in the Olympic Games.

The surf board's profile or cut determines how it surfs on the wave.

Who first stood on a surfboard?

Surfing was first enjoyed by the Polynesian islanders of the Pacific Ocean. The earliest description of someone surfing was written in Hawaii in 1779. Hawaiians used wooden boards more than 5 m long. Interest in surfing was revived in Australia and the United States, and world championships were first held in 1964.

Which is the fastest swimming stroke?

Of the four strokes in competitive swimming (breaststroke, backstroke, crawl and butterfly), the crawl is the fastest, followed by the butterfly. In competitive swimming, some races are designated 'freestyle', but all the top swimmers choose the crawl. The most widely used strokes by 19th-century swimmers were the breaststroke and sidestroke. Butterfly was officially recognized for use in racing in 1952.

What is a trimaran?

A trimaran is a sailing boat with three hulls. Trimarans and the twin-hulled catamarans were developed from the outrigger canoes used in the Pacific. Their appearance would have startled competitors in the first yacht race, between King Charles II and his brother James, Duke of York in 1661 on the River Thames. The original yachts were Dutch sailing boats.

The centre hull of a trimaran has the mast and crew compartment; the two other hulls provide extra stability at high speed.

All swimming strokes call for strong use of arm and leg muscles. This swimmer is using the butterfly stroke.

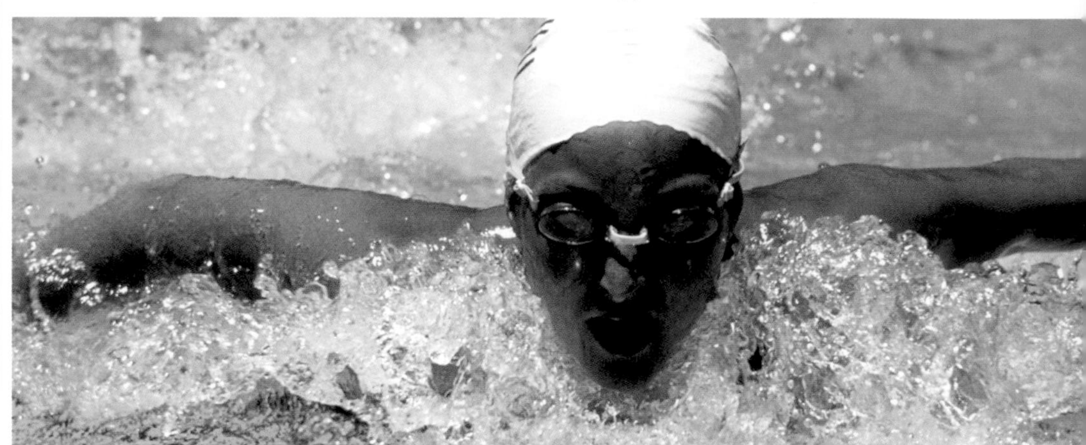

On snow and **in water**

Skiing and snowboarding

The two main forms of ski-racing are Alpine and Nordic. Alpine skiing is done on a downhill slope, sometimes with gates to twist through (a slalom event). Competitors set off one at a time and are timed to see who is fastest. Nordic skiing takes place across country, and includes ski-jumping, where skiers zoom down a slope and leap off the end of a ramp. Snowboarding combines skiing, surfing and skateboarding on a stubby board that flips across the snow, enabling the rider to perform stunts in the air.

Many aerial manoeuvres achieved in snowboarding are inspired by skateboarding techniques.

Skiing **terms**

Basket – ring at the end of the ski pole.
Bindings – fastenings holding ski boot to the ski.
Fall line – direct route down a slope.
Mogul – a bump in the slope.
Schussing – skiing straight down a slope.
Traversing – skiing across a slope.
Wedge or snow plough – stopping manoeuvre, bringing the front ends of the skis together in a V-shape.

A waterskier can skim over the water at speeds of up to 160 km/h.

Skiers hold long sticks, called ski-poles, to help them to steer and control.

What is the difference between a kayak and a canoe?

A kayak paddler uses a two-bladed paddle, whereas a canoeist has a single-bladed paddle. Modern canoes and kayaks originated among the Native Americans and Inuit peoples of North America, who used canoes for transportation. Canoeing as a sport dates from 1866 and has been an Olympic event since 1936. In a modern canoe it is possible to turn upside down and roll upright again without coming to any harm.

The kayak paddle must hit the water at such an angle as to provide the correct stroke to propel the kayak forward.

Who was the first waterskier?

The first waterskier was an American named Ralph Samuelson who gave the first exhibition of ski jumping from a ramp in 1925. Waterskiers hold on to a tow-rope and are pulled along on water skis, which are wider than snow skis, by a motorboat. The skier does stunts, slalom turns in and out of obstacles or jumps up a sloping ramp.

When were snow skis first used?

Ancient skis over 4,000 years old have been found in Scandinavia, where people made wooden skis to get around on during the long, snowy winters. In 1843, the first skiing competition was held in Norway. Modern skis are made of plastic, metal or fibreglass, but the basic principles are unchanged: the novice skier has to learn how to start, turn, and stop. At top speed, a downhill skier can whizz along at up to over 240 km/h.

Safety rules **for swimmers**

- Never swim alone in a lake or the sea.
- Beware of currents in the sea.
- Obey 'no-swimming' signs, warning flags or advice from lifeguards.
- Never dive into water without knowing how deep it is.
- Never dive into a pool close to other swimmers.
- Avoid swimming straight after eating.

Most swimming races start with a dive from one end of the pool.

Key **dates**

36 BC Japan is the first country to stage swimming races.
1888 First World Championships (unofficial) are held in Australia.
1896 Swimming is one of the events in the revived Olympic Games.
1900 Water polo introduced to the Olympics.
1904 Diving (for men) introduced to the Olympics.
1973 First swimming world championships.
1984 Synchronized swimming is admitted to the Olympics.

People probably first played ball games thousands of years ago. Inflated pigs' bladders were used as balls in the Middle Ages, and children used curved sticks for early versions of cricket and golf. Schools and colleges began organizing ball games as part of formal education in the 19th century, leading to the amazing growth in professional ball-sports across the world today.

Which team sport attracts the most spectators?

The world's most popular spectator sport is soccer, which is played and watched on every continent. Only in the USA is professional soccer not the leading team game. Soccer originated from violent medieval football games, but was organized with rules, leagues and professional teams in the 19th century. The World Cup, held every four years, is the biggest international soccer tournament. The international governing body, FIFA, was set up in 1904.

Soccer is money-making entertainment, especially in Europe and South America.

How fast does a pitcher throw a baseball?

A baseball pitcher can throw the ball (which weighs 148 g) at up to 160 km/h. Baseball was first played by modern rules in New Jersey, USA in 1846, although a similar rounders-like game had been played long before this in the UK. Professional clubs first appeared in 1871 and the national league was established in 1876. The winners of the two main US leagues, the National and the American, meet every year in the seven-game World Series.

Baseball catchers wear protective clothing to shield against the impact of the ball.

Which king played tennis?

The monarch best-known for playing tennis is England's Henry VIII who, as a young man, was an expert at real (royal) tennis, which was played on a walled court. The game later moved outside and rules for 'lawn tennis' were drawn up in the 1800s. The first Wimbledon Championship, the oldest of the 'Grand Slams', was held in 1877. The most successful men's players at Wimbledon are Bjorn Borg (five singles titles, 1976–80) and Pete Sampras (seven singles titles, 1993–2000). Martina Navratilova won her 20th Wimbledon title in 2003, equalling the women's record held by Billie-Jean King.

Ball **facts**

Catching the ball in a net

Lacrosse is a minority game among the world's ball games. First played by Native Americans in Canada, when as many as 1,000 players practically fought one another in a game, it is now played mostly in schools and colleges.

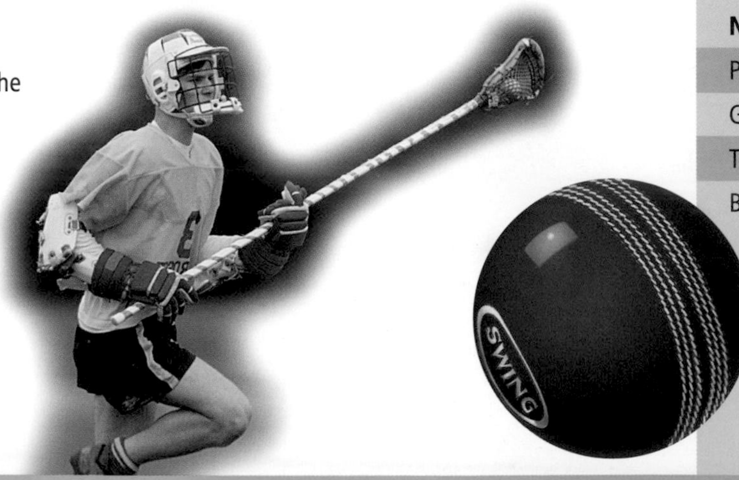

Lacrosse players wield a netting pocket on the end of a stick (the crosse), with which to catch and throw the ball.

Fastest **balls**

Name	Speed
Pelota ball	300 km/h
Golf ball	270 km/h
Tennis ball	220 km/h
Baseball / cricket ball	160 km/h

The speed of a cricket ball depends on how it is bowled: it can be bowled fast or spun slowly.

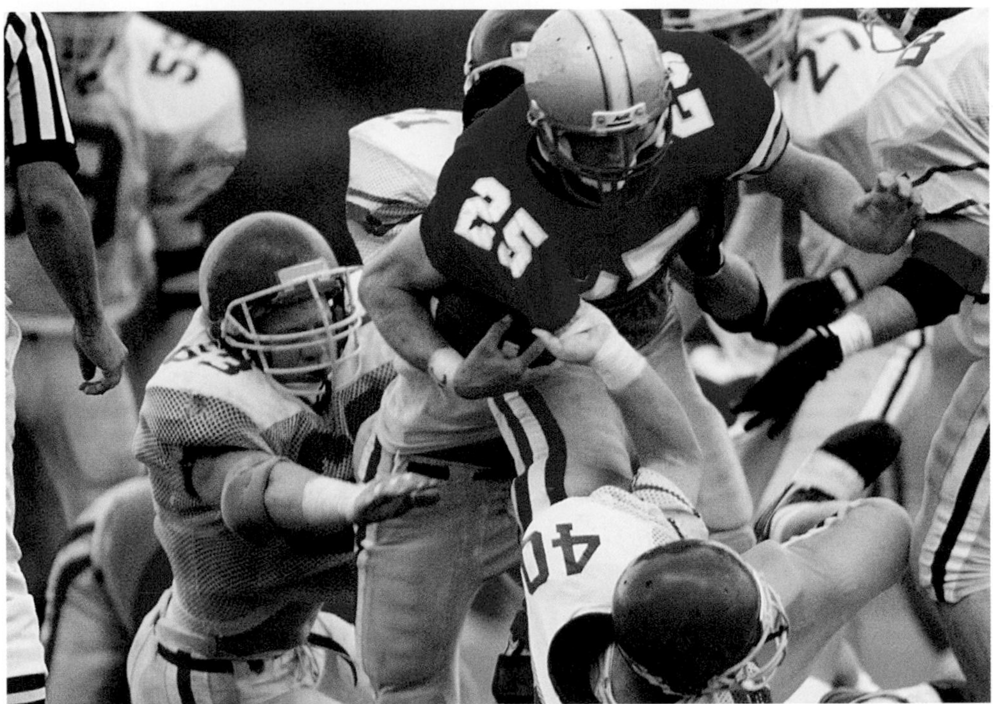

Players grapple for the ball during American football, which requires them to wear padding.

Where was golf first played?

The earliest mention of golf is in a Scottish law of 1457, banning the game. Games similar to golf were played much earlier. The oldest golf championship is Britain's 'Open', first played in 1860. The objective of golf is to get the ball into a small hole on the 'green' in as few putts as possible.

In which sport does it help to be exceptionally tall?

Basketball – very tall players can more easily send the ball into the net (basket) to score points. Basketball was invented in the USA in 1891 as an indoor winter team game. Two teams of five players try to score points by tossing the ball into the opposing team's basket. Players must not run with the ball and have time limits for passing.

Which game is played on a grid-iron?

The grid-iron is the pitch on which American football is played. Developed by university students in the 19th century, the game is a spin-off from soccer and rugby. The pitch contains lines that cross the field every 4.6 m from one sideline to the other. Two teams of 11 players compete for the Super Bowl, which is played each year by the champions of the two main leagues: the National Football Conference (NFC) and the American Football Conference (AFC).

The ball must drop into or through basket from above to score. The ball can be bounced into the basket off the backboard.

Playing pelota

Pelota is a ball game that originated in northern Spain. It usually involves two players (known as pelotari) or two teams each comprising two players, who use either their bare hands, a racket or a cesta (curved wooden basket) to hit the ball onto the opposing side's wall. There are seven forms of the game in total, each with differing rules.

Pelotari can hit the ball using a cesta, which is made from chesnut and willow.

Soccer **records**

The first World Cup, held in Uruguay in 1930, was won by Uruguay. Brazil is the only country to have appeared in every World Cup final. Brazil are the only team to have won the World Cup five times.

Record	Answer
Most famous soccer player	Pelè of Brazil
Britain's first soccer knight	Sir Stanley Matthews
Biggest soccer tournament	World Cup
Oldest tournament	FA Cup
First women's world championship	1991
Highest score in UK	36–0 (Arbroath v Bon Acord in 1885, a Scottish Cup Match)

TRACK AND FIELD EVENTS

The first people to take running seriously and compete against one another were the ancient Greeks. Track and field athletics as we know them began in the 19th century in schools and colleges in Europe and North America. These events play a big part in the Olympic Games, and there are also regular world and regional championships. Track races and some field events can also take place indoors.

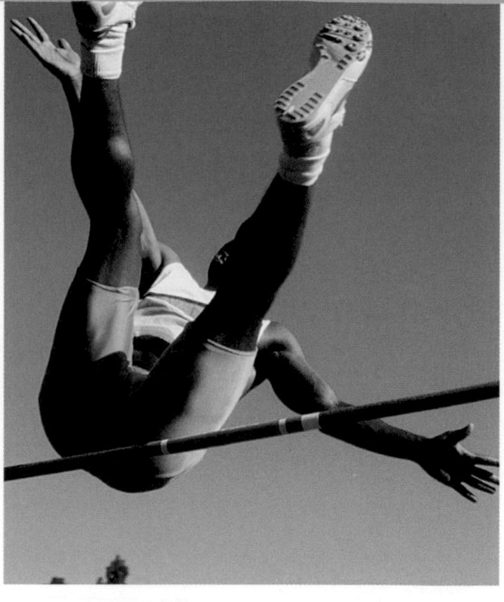

As sprinters cross the finish line, they push their heads forward so that the winner is clearly visible.

How fast can a sprinter run?

A male sprinter can speed down the 100-m straight in about 9.8 sec – a speed of just over 40 km/h. This is slower than a horse, which can sprint at 56 km/h, or a greyhound (67 km/h), but faster than a swimmer (about 8 km/h). The 100-m sprint is the shortest outdoor race in athletics; indoor sprints are 60-m dashes.

How many hurdle races are there?

In track and field events, three races involve runners jumping over barriers called hurdles. The shortest is the 110-m hurdles race (100-m for women) in which competitors aim to stride over hurdles, which measure 107 m high for men and 84 m high for women. For both men and women, in the one-lap 400-m hurdle race the hurdles are lower. In the steeplechase, which is more than 3,000 m, athletes jump over a wooden hurdle and leap over a waterjump.

Which long jumper astonished the world?

Bob Beamon (USA) set an amazing world long jump record in 1968 at the Mexico City Olympics. The high altitude caused thin air (a lack of oxygen), making Beamon's leap of 8.9 m even more amazing. Beamon had shattered the previous world record and no jumper had ever jumped more than 8.5 m. Beamon's record lasted until 1991 when Mike Powell (USA) broke it by 5 cm.

A male hurdler must jump clear of a barrier at least 1 m high.

On your **marks...**

Carl Lewis, winner of ten world championship medals.

Jesse Owens was the star of the 1936 Olympics, winning long jump, sprint and relay.

Amazing **track facts**

- Jesse Owens (USA) won four gold medals at the 1936 Olympics and held seven world records.
- Emil Zátopek (Czech Republic) won four gold medals at Olympic Games and held ten world records.
- Al Oerter (USA) won the Olympic discus gold medal four times.
- Roger Bannister (UK) was the first man to run a mile in under four minutes, in 1954.
- Raymond Ewry (USA) won a record ten Olympic medals between 1900 and 1908 for jumping.

A javelin thrower runs about 12 very quick strides and accelerates to 7 m/sec, gaining momentum for the throw. A throw is only valid if the javelin touches the ground with the tip first. Javelin throwing has featured in the Olympic Games since 1908.

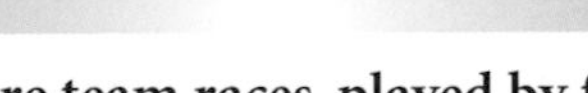

What is a relay race?

Relays are team races, played by four runners in each team. Each runner carries a baton, which must be passed to the next runner at a changeover point. The most common relays in track athletics are the 4 x 100 m and the 4 x 400 m, for both men and women. In a baton relay race, dropping the baton means the whole team is disqualified from the event.

In a baton relay race the next team member must start running before the previous runner has handed the baton to him. It is the baton, not the runner, that is timed. The baton is made from wood or metal and weighs about 50 g.

What are field events?

Field events include throwing and jumping. There are four throwing events: javelin, discus, shotput and hammer. The four jumping events are long jump, triple jump, high jump and pole vault. Pole vault athletes use a fibreglass pole to help lift themselves over a bar, which is more than 6 m high.

The triple jump involves three stages: a hop, a step and a two-footed jump.

1 Gaining height

2 Gaining momentum

3 Gaining speed

4 Landing on sand with both feet as far forward as possible

- Paavo Nurmi (Finland) won five gold medals for running, in the 1925 Olympics.
- Irena Szewinska (Poland) won medals at four successive games from 1964 to 1976.
- Barbara Jones (USA) was just 15 years old when she won a gold medal in the 4 x 100 m relay at the 1952 Olympics – the youngest track gold medallist.
- Carl Lewis (USA) won ten world championship medals, eight of them gold. His events were long jump, 100 m and 4 x 100 m relay. He also won eight Olympic gold medals between 1984 and 1992.

Top distance runners like Britain's Paula Radcliffe put in many hours and kilometres of training.

The earliest sport on wheels was chariot racing, which was enjoyed by ancient Egyptians and Romans. In the 19th century, bicycles were raced, and from 1885 the motorcar and motorcycle were soon used for racing. Today, motorsport in its various forms, on purpose-built racing circuits and on roads, is followed avidly by fans across the world.

British racing champion Stirling Moss drove 84 different vehicles during his career.

Where was the first motor race?

The first race for cars was in France in 1895. Emile Levassor won, driving his car at an average speed of just over 24 km/h. The race from Paris to Bordeaux and back covered 1,178 km. Grand Prix racing began in 1906, also in France, and is now held at circuits across the world. Today's Grand Prix cars travel more than ten times faster than in 1895.

Competitors take part in events such as indoor sprints, pursuit and time trials on steep tracks and outdoor road races.

Which is the most famous cycle race?

The Tour de France, which was first raced in 1903. It is the biggest event for racing cyclists and takes 21 days to complete. Each stage has a separate winner but the overall winner receives the coveted yellow jersey. Cycle racing began in 1868 and the first world championships were staged in 1903. Cycling has been an Olympic sport since the first modern Olympics in 1896.

Speedway bikes have no brakes so riders must use their feet as they slide around bends, sending up showers of dirt.

What is speedway?

Speedway, also known as dirt-track racing, is a form of motorcycle racing. Modern speedway dates from the 1920s in Australia and the first world championships were held in 1936. Unlike other forms of motorcycle racing, such as scrambling or motocross, which take place on 'natural' outdoor circuits, speedway riders compete around an oval track. During each race, which lasts for four laps, the four riders taking part slide into the tight bends.

Motorsport **facts**

Key **dates**

1895 First organized car race in France.
1906 First Grand Prix race, at Le Mans, France.
1911 First Indianapolis 500 in the USA.
1920 Grand Prix races first held outside France.
1923 First 24-hour race for sports cars at Le Mans.
1936 First organized stock car races in the USA.
1960s Rear-engined cars take over from front-engined cars in Grand Prix races.

Motorcycle racers compete over winding circuits.

Cyclo-cross riders have to negotiate hills, water and mud.

Motocross riders become airborne on a 'scramble' over bumps and bends.

What is the difference between a rally and a race?

During a car rally, cars set off at intervals and are timed on each section. During a race, a number of cars start in ranks from a grid and race around a circuit with bends and straights. Rallies cover several thousand kilometres and take several days to complete. They are often held across wild country: one rally is held in East Africa, another across the Sahara. The most famous rally is the Monte Carlo Rally. Car races include the Grand Prix races held in various countries, the Indianapolis 500 in the USA and the Le Mans 24-hour race in France.

Stock cars look like wrecks but keep going at full speed.

Drag racers have huge rear wheels to get them moving, and aerofoils to keep the wheels on the ground as the car accelerates.

A rally car is a modified production car, which can be driven over extremely challenging terrain, such as muddy hillsides, that tests both machine and driver.

What are stock-car and drag racing?

Stock cars are known as hot rods or old bangers, which have been modified for a crash-and-bang race around a large, speedway-sized track. Drag cars are designed to speed down a 400 m long track, at speeds of up to 500 km/h. A race lasts less than 10 sec and only two cars compete each time, until one car is left victorious. In both stock-car and drag racing, collisions are frequent and many of the cars end up looking like battered wrecks.

Amazing **facts**

- The oldest motorcycle races are the Isle of Man TT races, first held in 1907.
- Specially modified cycles have been pedalled at more than 268 km/h – behind a windshield provided by a car in front.
- More than 31,000 people took part in the London to Brighton bike ride in 1988.
- The oldest world motor racing champion was the Argentinian Juan Manuel Fangio, who won the last of his five titles in 1957 at the age of 46.
- The longest car rally was in 1977 from London to Sydney – a distance of 31,107 km.
- Skateboarding is fairly new, in wheely-sport terms, and fairly slow. Even so, skateboard experts can put on a startling show of acrobatics on wheels.

A GT car is a faster-than-normal version of a standard model.

Grand **Prix drivers**

Name	Nationality	Number of wins
Michael Shumacher	German	53
Alain Prost	French	51
Ayrton Senna	Brazilian	41
Nigel Mansell	British	31
Jackie Stewart	British	27
Jim Clarke	British	25
Niki Lauder	Australian	25
Juan Fangio	Argentinian	24
Graham Hill	British	2
Damon Hill	British	1

People have always enjoyed playing games. As town life began to develop more than 5,000 years ago, people played board games and games of chance, using dice or marked pieces, such as dominoes. The ancient Egyptians enjoyed chariot racing and wrestling, and Greek athletes took part in the Olympic Games more than 3,000 years ago. Rules for many modern games such as tennis, rugby, football and baseball were established in the 1800s. Some professional sports stars today are among the highest-paid people in the world.

Why did Romans flock to the Colosseum?

Crowds flocked to the Colosseum, a stadium in ancient Rome, to watch 'the games'. The games were not sports in the modern sense but lavish shows, during which animals and people met bloody deaths. People came to watch fights between gladiators (specially-trained fighters) or between men and wild animals. There were even mock hunts and mock sea-battles, for which the arena was flooded.

Philippides ran from Marathon to Athens, then collapsed and died.

In Rome's Colosseum, the spectators sat in circular tiers that rose in height around the arena, which was built like a circus ring. The structure itself was made of concrete, which was invented by the Romans.

How did the Marathon race get its name?

The Marathon race takes its name from a battle in 490 BC between the Greeks and Persians on the Plain of Marathon, in Greece. After the Greek victory, a runner named Philippides ran 24 mi (38 km) to Athens, gasped 'Rejoice, we have won' and died of exhaustion. The Marathon has been set at its present distance of over 26 mi 385 yd (43 km) since 1908, and is run in various cities. Thousands of amateurs as well as top athletes take part in popular races, such as the London Marathon.

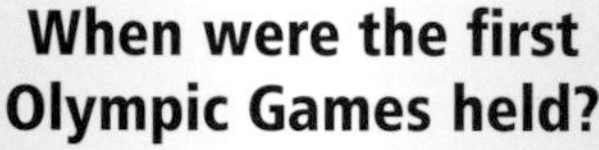

When were the first Olympic Games held?

The first Olympic Games were held in ancient Greece, in 776 BC and continued to be held there until AD 393. In 1896, the first modern Games were held in Athens, Greece, with just nine events. The Winter Olympics began in 1924. The Olympics have been held every four years since 1896, except during wartime (1916, 1940 and 1944).

All about **games and sport**

Key **dates**

1299 Bowling club recorded in Southampton, England.
1330 First known references to, and pictures of, hockey.
1544 Earliest mention of billiards.
1620 *Mayflower* pilgrims play darts.
1657 Earliest known golf match played between Scotland and England.
1744 First cricket rules were formed.
1846 First recorded baseball game under modern rules.
1860s Badminton first played.
1863 English Football Association (FA) formed.
1865 Queensberry Rules for boxing were established.
1874 Lawn tennis invented, as 'sphairistike' (Greek for 'ball').
1875 Earliest mention of snooker.
1898 First international cross-country race.

Greyhound racing is a modern version of ancient contests, such as hare-coursing, between hunting dogs. The mechanical hare was first used in 1919.

Which country has the fattest wrestlers?

Japan, where sumo wrestling is practised by wrestlers of huge body weight, up to 267 kg. Sumo is at least 2,000 years old, and has strict rules and ceremonies. Being very fat is an advantage, since the object of the wrestler is to push his opponent out of the circular ring. Any hold is permitted, unlike Greco-Roman wrestling, where the wrestler cannot seize his opponent below the hips or use his legs. In freestyle wrestling, almost all moves are permitted.

The heavier the sumo wrestler, the more strength they have to push their opponent.

The goaltender is heavily padded during an ice-hockey game to prevent serious injury.

Which is the fastest team game?

In a game of ice hockey, the rubber puck can whizz over the ice at more than 160 km/h. A form of hockey on ice was played in the Netherlands in the 1500s, but modern ice hockey has its origins in 19th-century Canada. Each ice hockey team is made up of six players, and substitutes are allowed during the game, which has three periods each lasting 20 minutes.

Who first played polo?

Polo began among the horsemen of central Asia and Persia (now Iran) some 4,000 years ago. The polo 'ball' was sometimes the head of a slain enemy! Modern polo dates from the 1860s, when British army officers saw the game played in India. Polo is played on a field 274 m long by riders who wield mallets whilst mounted on ponies. The aim of the game is to score a goal by hitting a ball through the opponents' goal posts.

Training a polo pony to twist and turn at speed takes about six months.

Amazing **Olympic facts**

Record	Date	Place
First modern Olympics	1896	Athens, Greece
First women medallists	1900	Paris, France
First Winter Games	1924	Chamonix, France
First Olympic village built	1932	Los Angeles, USA
First torch-lighting ceremony	1936	Berlin, Germany
Mark Spitz wins seven gold medals	1972	Munich, Germany
Carl Lewis wins eight gold medals	1984 / 1992	Los Angeles, USA and Barcelona, Spain
Marion Jones wins five medals	2000	Sydney, Australia
Most events ever held (300)	2000	Sydney, Australia

An early 20th-century golf championship player preparing to drive, watched by attentive spectators in the Open Championship, which was first played in Britain in 1860, at Prestwick in Scotland.

QUIZ TIME

Why not test your knowledge on arts, sports and entertainment! Try answering these questions to find out how much you know about music, movies, artists, literature, sports, designers, architecture and much more. Questions are grouped into the subject areas covered within the pages of this book. See how much you remember and discover how much more you can learn.

Music

1 Which trumpet-playing jazz singer was known as 'Satchmo'?

2 What type of instrument are the violin, cello and guitar examples of?

3 Which classical composer went deaf whilst writing his fifth symphony, but went on to write four more after that?

Art

4 What kind of flowers do we associate with the painter Claude Monet?

5 Name the English artist who is famed for painting swimming pools?

6 In which century was the artist Michaelangelo born?

Design

8 From which country did Charles Rennie Mackintosh originate?

9 In tailoring terms, what does 'bespoke' mean?

10 Which designer was made famous through the publication of a book entitled *The Gentleman and Cabinet Maker's Director*?

Architecture

11 What name is given to the central stone of an arch?

12 What do you call the tall, decorated wooden pillars carved by Native Americans?

13 Which opera house was opened in 1973 and looks like yachts in full sail?

7 Which famous composer was the first to arrange musical instruments into the four main groups: strings, woodwinds, brass and percussion?

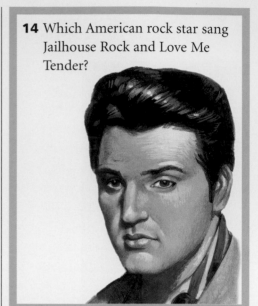

14 Which American rock star sang Jailhouse Rock and Love Me Tender?

Performing Arts

15 In which Italian city did the Shakespearean merchant Antonio ply his trade?

16 Which London theatre, opened in 1871, was named after Queen Victoria's husband?

17 Is Don Alfonso a leading character in *Aida*, *Cosi Fan Tutti* or the *Barber of Seville*?

TV and Cinema

18 Which television street features the characters of Bert, Ernie and the Cookie Monster?

19 What kind of animal is Disney's Dumbo?

20 Where does Bart Simpson live?

Literature

21 Which American author wrote the classic novel *The Scarlett Letter*?

22 In mythology, how many eyes did the Cyclops have?

23 Which Shakespeare play is often referred to as the Scottish play?

Myths and Legends

24 In Greek mythology, Eros was the god of what?

25 Which Greek mythological hero killed the gorgon Medusa?

26 Who is the Greek goddess of love?

History of Culture

27 Which Italian artist painted a mural called *The Last Supper* around 1495?

28 With which art movement do you associate Salvador Dali?

29 From which art gallery was the *Mona Lisa* stolen in 1911?

Water and Snow Sports

31 Crouch roll and poke fall are both types of what?

32 Which American won seven gold medals at the 1972 Olympic Games?

33 Is the alternative name for cross-country skiing: alpine skiing, Nordic skiing or Viking skiing?

Ball Sports

34 How often is the football World Cup held?

35 The Super Bowl is a trophy played for in which sport?

36 For which national football team did Pelè play?

Track and Field Events

37 How many laps of the track are run in an outdoor 400-m race?

38 In athletics track races, what does the ringing of a bell signify?

39 Which American sprinter set a world record for the 100 m in 1999?

Sport on Wheels

40 Which Frenchman was the first Formula One driver to register 50 Grand Prix wins?

41 Which Scottish driver won the Monaco Grand Prix in May 2002?

42 Irishman Stephen Roche won which sporting event in 1987?

History of Sport

43 Which country hosted the 2002 Winter Olympics?

44 Which martial art made its Olympic debut at the 2000 Sydney Games?

45 In 1994, which West Indian batsman scored 501 not out in one innings?

30 Who wrote *Gulliver's Travels*, the story of a man who travelled to places where he was among giants, or was a giant himself?

Answers

1 Louis Armstrong
2 Stringed instruments
3 Beethoven
4 Water Lilies
5 David Hockney
6 15th century
7 Haydn
8 Scotland
9 Made to measure
10 Thomas Chippendale
11 Keystone
12 Totem poles
13 Sydney Opera House
14 Elvis Presley
15 Venice
16 The Royal Albert Hall
17 *Cosi Fan Tutti*
18 Sesame Street
19 Elephant
20 Springfield
21 Nathaniel Hawthorn
22 One
23 *Macbeth*
24 Love
25 Perseus
26 Aphrodite
27 Leonardo da Vinci
28 Surrealism
29 The Louvre in Paris
30 Jonathan Swift
31 Diving style
32 Mark Spitz
33 Nordic
34 Every four years
35 American football
36 Brazil
37 One
38 The runners are on their final lap
39 Maurice Green
40 Alain Prost
41 David Coulthard
42 Tour de France
43 USA
44 Taekwondo
45 Brian Lara

INDEX

Page numbers in **bold** refer to main subjects; page numbers in *italics* refer to illustrations.

The publishers would like to thank the following artists who have contributed to this book:
Steve Caldwell, Jim Channell, Peter Dennis, Nicholas Forder, Luigi Galante Studios, Terry Grose, Alan Hancocks, Sally Holmes, Richard Hook, John James, Maltings, Janos Marffy, Chris Odgers, Rachel Phillips, Terry Riley, Martin Sanders, Mike Sanders, Peter Sarson, Roger Smith, Gwen Tourret, Mike White

The publishers wish to thank the following sources for the photographs used in this book:
Argos p13 (b/r); AFP/GETTY IMAGES p16 (b/r); Pictorialpress.com (b/r); Pictorialpress.com p17 (b/r); Volkwagen p19 (b); Warners/Pictorialpress.com (b/r); Pictorialpress.com p20 (c/r); Jim Sugar/Corbis p29 (b); Corr/AFP/GETTY IMAGES p30 (b/c); Damien Meyer/AFP/GETTY IMAGES p31 (b/r); Joel Saget/AFP/GETTY IMAGES p32 (c/r); Neil Brake/AFP/GETTY IMAGES p33 (b/c)

All other photographs are from:
Castrol, CMCD, Corbis, Corel, Digitalvision, ILN, PhotoDisc